To

on the occasion of

Date

This edition copyright © 1995 Lion Publishing
Illustrations copyright © 1995 William Geldart

Published by
Lion Publishing plc
Sandy Lane West, Oxford, England
ISBN 0 7459 3360 2
Albatross Books Pty Ltd
PO Box 320, Sutherland, NSW 2232, Australia
ISBN 0 7324 1322 2

First edition 1995
10 9 8 7 6 5 4 3 2 1

All rights reserved

Acknowledgments
Illustrations by William Geldart

A catalogue record for this book is available
from the British Library

Printed and bound in Singapore

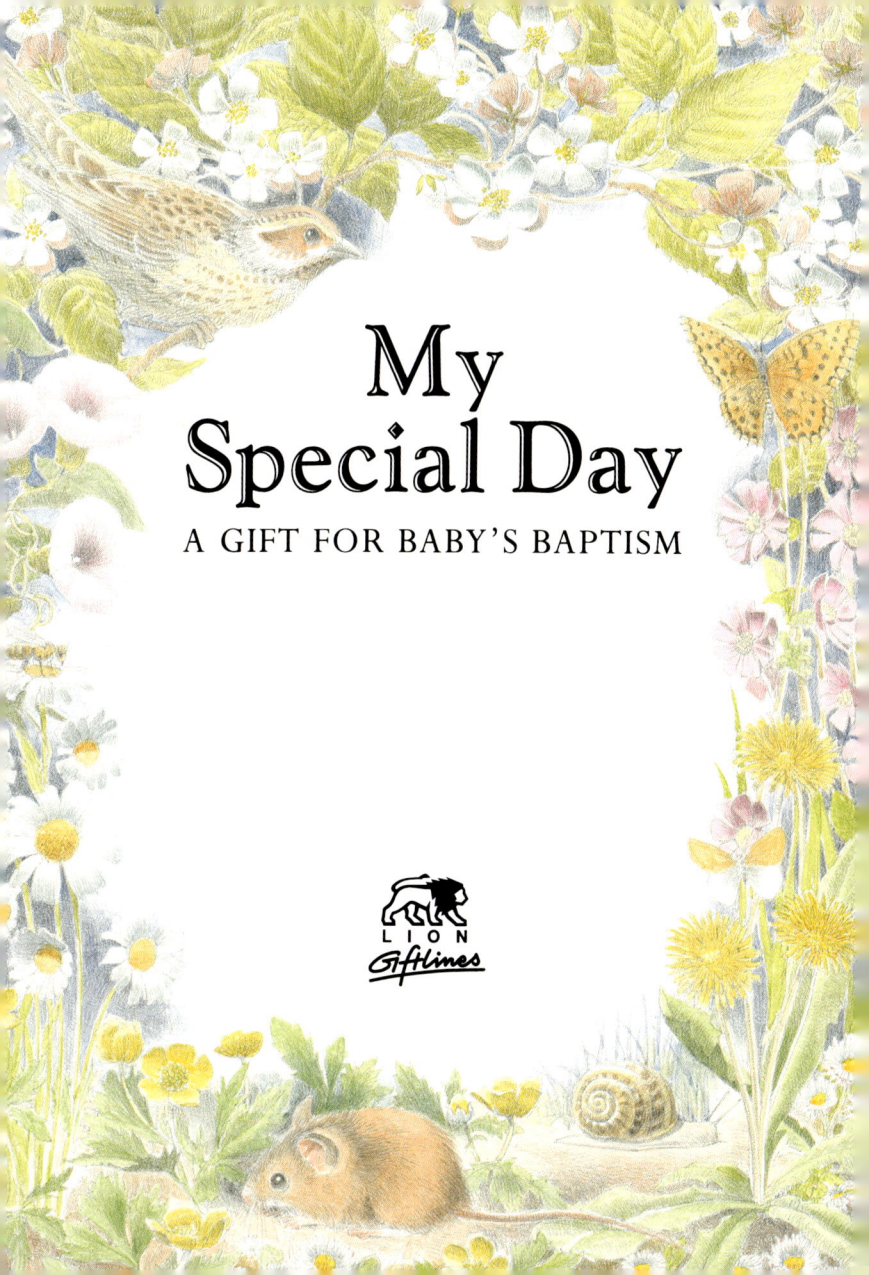

My Special Day

A GIFT FOR BABY'S BAPTISM

LION
Giftlines

Introduction

This book is a gift with a long life. Its aim is both to mark baby's first special occasion – his or her baptism or christening day – and to become a treasured possession as the years go by.

The day is important to you as a parent because of what it represents. It's a family celebration, the opportunity to thank God for the miracle of a new life and to entrust your baby to his love and care. It is an occasion at which to make promises on your child's behalf, in the certainty that God knows and loves your baby every bit as much as you do.

Later on, this book will help you to share the significance of this special occasion with your growing child. The questions will help you to personalise the book by adding in the extra details that made your day special. As you share the prayers together, your child will begin to feel part of God's family.

We hope the book will bring joy and happiness to both you and your child and be a lasting record of an important event in your child's life.

NOTE TO PARENTS

The text assumes a rather traditional family structure, but this may not meet your own situation. Please adjust as necessary.

We have used the title 'minister' but other titles such as priest, vicar, rector or pastor should be substituted where appropriate to your situation.

He/she has been used to allow you to personalize the prayers for your child.

My special day

When I was born, Mum and Dad were so happy that they thanked everybody; the nurses, the doctors and the midwife. And they thanked God too.

As soon as I was old enough they took me to church. It was my very special day and it was called my baptism. Another word for it is my christening, but they mean the same thing.

What did I wear on the day?

God's family

I was born into a family. We belong to each other, we look after and love one another. Sometimes we may argue, or do things that make each other unhappy, but we still love each other.

On my special day, I joined another family, too – God's family. It is sometimes called the Church and it includes everyone who loves God and his son Jesus.

Where is my church?

What happened on my special day

My parents took me to the church. There were lots of people there. They sang songs and talked to God in prayers. My parents and godparents promised to pray for me, to teach me and to show me how to be a good member of God's family.

My godparents are very important to me. They love me and will help me as I grow up.

Who are my godparents?

The baptism

Next the minister held me in his/her arms, took some water or some oil and made a cross-shape on my forehead.

The minister said: 'I sign you with the cross, the sign of Christ.'

The cross is the sign of Jesus. It is like a badge that says I belong to him.

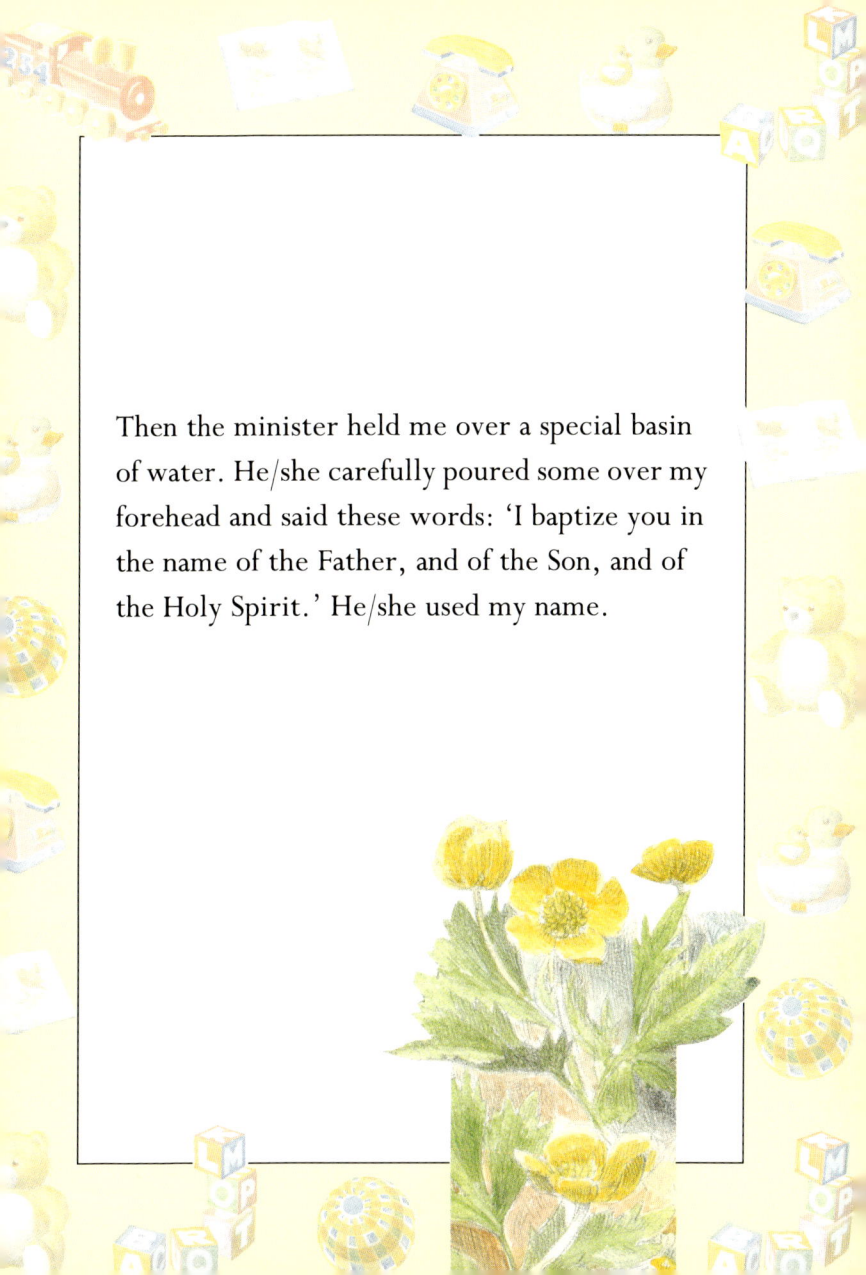

Then the minister held me over a special basin of water. He/she carefully poured some over my forehead and said these words: 'I baptize you in the name of the Father, and of the Son, and of the Holy Spirit.' He/she used my name.

A candle

After the baptism, the minister gave me a lighted candle. I was too small to hold it, so someone held it for me. The minister said: 'This is to show that you have passed from darkness to light. Shine as a light in the world to the glory of God the Father.'

Who held the candle for me?

After that, everyone in my new family, the Church, said: 'We welcome you.' They prayed some more prayers and sang more songs.

We didn't go straight home. Everyone wanted to see me.

My family and friends talked together for a long time!

What else did we do that day?

Some prayers we prayed

This one was for me:

*Heavenly Father, in your love
you have called us to know you,
led us to trust you,
and bound our life with yours.
Surround this child with your love;
protect him/her from evil;
fill him/her with your Holy Spirit;
and receive him/her into the family of your Church;
that he/she may walk with us in the way of Christ
and grow in the knowledge of your love.
Amen*

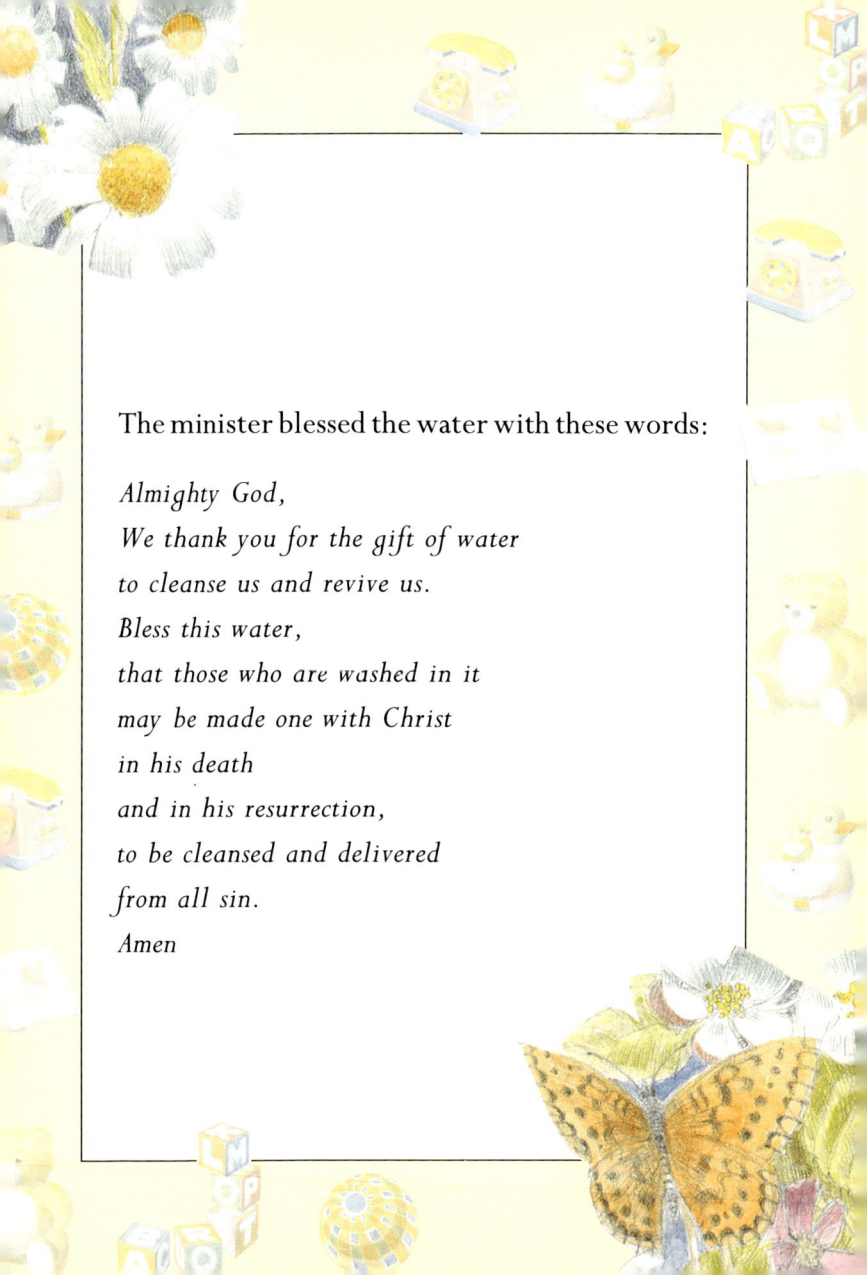

The minister blessed the water with these words:

Almighty God,
We thank you for the gift of water
to cleanse us and revive us.
Bless this water,
that those who are washed in it
may be made one with Christ
in his death
and in his resurrection,
to be cleansed and delivered
from all sin.
Amen

We prayed for my parents:

Heavenly Father, we pray for the parents of this child; give them the spirit of wisdom and love, that their home may reflect the joy of your eternal kingdom. Amen

And for everyone in God's family:

Almighty God, we thank you for our fellowship in the household of faith with all those who have been baptized in your name. Keep us faithful to our baptism, and so make us ready for that day when the whole creation shall be made perfect in your Son, our Saviour Jesus Christ. Amen

My name

I was not given my name at my baptism. My parents did that, soon after I was born. They wrote it on a piece of paper called a birth certificate. But my baptism was the first time that my name was heard by lots of people.

What does my birth certificate look like?

My name is written at the beginning of this book. The first name is called a Christian name. It is my own name. The last name is called a surname. All my family members have the same name. It tells everyone which family we belong to.

What are my mum and dad's Christian names?

The church

God's family has a name, too. We are called Christians. It comes from the name Christ.

This name was given to Jesus to show that he was God's chosen Son. People soon began to call him Jesus Christ and they called his followers Christ-ians, or Christians.

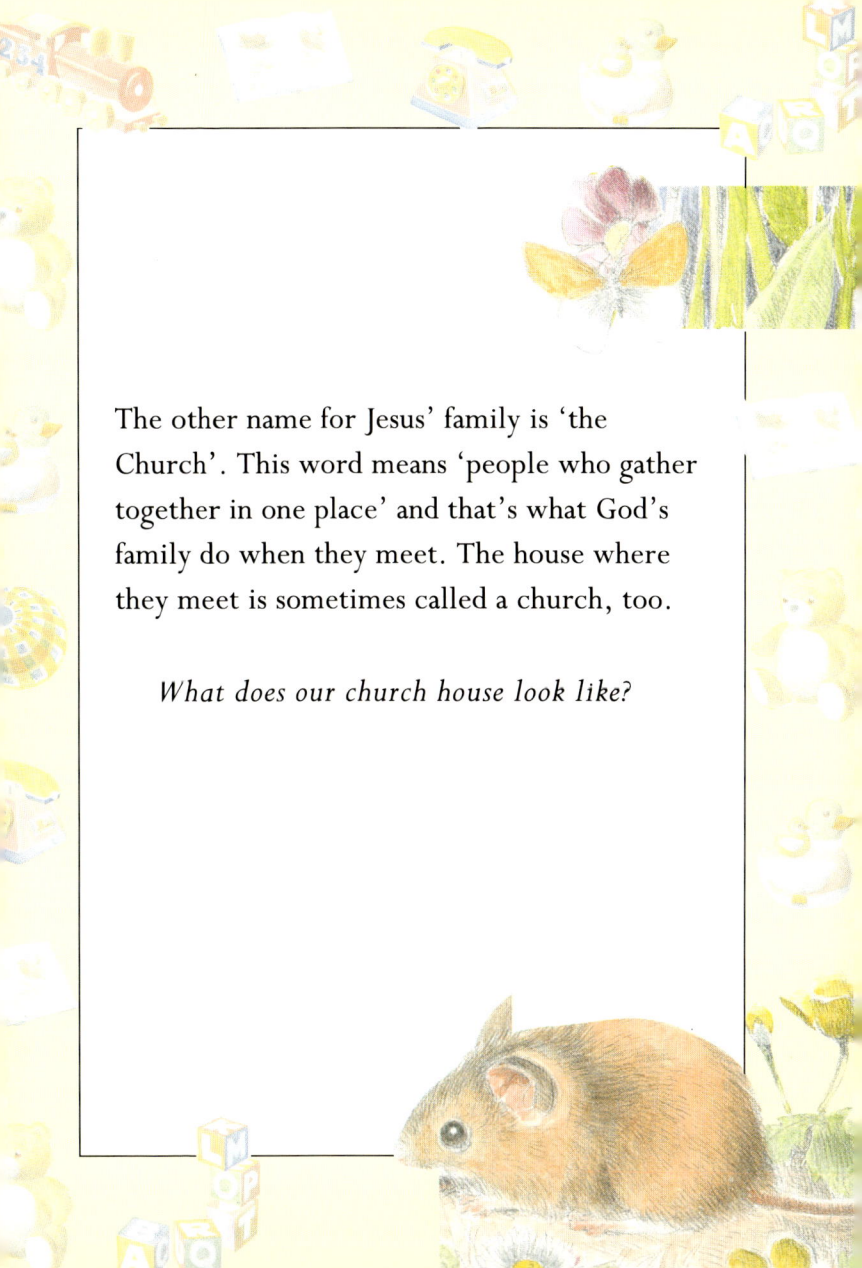

The other name for Jesus' family is 'the Church'. This word means 'people who gather together in one place' and that's what God's family do when they meet. The house where they meet is sometimes called a church, too.

What does our church house look like?

What Jesus said about children

Jesus loved children. One day, he was sitting telling stories, when some mothers brought their children to see him. Jesus' friends said, 'Don't bother Jesus now, he's busy.' But Jesus said, 'Let the children come to me. Don't stop them. They are just the sort of people I want in my family.' Then he took them in his arms, put his hands on their heads and prayed for them.

Jesus gave us his own prayer to pray. It is written here in simple language:

Our Father in heaven:
Your name is very special to us.
Be king of our hearts
so that we do what you want on earth
as they do in heaven.
Give us today the food we need.
Forgive us when we do wrong things,
and help us to forgive those who are unkind to us.
Please stop us from doing bad things,
and keep us safe from every danger.
Our hearts are yours.
You have all the power
and all the glory,
for ever and ever.
Amen

My prayers

Dear Jesus,
Thank you for my family,
my mum and dad
and my godparents.
Thank you for making me part of your own family
at my baptism.
Amen.

For my family
For my friends,
For your love that never ends.
Thank you heavenly Father.

Jesus, friend of little children,
Be a friend to me;
Take my hand and ever keep me
Close to thee.

A morning prayer

Father, we thank you for the night,
And for the pleasant morning light;
For rest and food and loving care,
And all that makes the day so fair.
Help us to do the things we should,
To be to others kind and good;
In all we do at work or play
To grow more loving every day.

At mealtimes

Thank you for the world so sweet,
Thank you for the food we eat,
Thank you for the birds that sing,
Thank you God for everything.

A night-time prayer

Jesus, tender Shepherd, hear me;
Bless your little lamb tonight;
Through the darkness please be near me;
Keep me safe till morning light.